Original title:
In the Mood

Copyright © 2024 Creative Arts Management OÜ
All rights reserved.

Author: Julian Montgomery
ISBN HARDBACK: 978-9916-88-888-9
ISBN PAPERBACK: 978-9916-88-889-6

Threads of Tranquility

In the hush of the dawn, soft whispers play,
Nature's lullaby calls the night into day.
Gentle winds weave through trees with grace,
Finding solace in this sacred space.

Clouds drift by like dreams in the air,
Colors meld softly in moments to share.
Stillness surrounds, a warm embrace,
Peace unfolds in nature's trace.

A Palette of Pleasures

Life's canvas paints joy in vibrant hues,
With laughter and love, we cannot lose.
With each stroke, we dance through the day,
A burst of color in every play.

Sunlit blossoms, fragrant and bright,
Whisper sweet secrets in soft morning light.
Each moment a brush, each touch a song,
In this masterpiece, we all belong.

Cascade of Sensations

Feel the rhythm of life, a flowing stream,
Every heartbeat echoes a tender dream.
Whispers of joy cascade like the rain,
Cleansing the spirit, washing the pain.

Within every heartbeat, a story unfolds,
Moments of wonder in memories hold.
Euphoria dances on a thrilling breeze,
Life's hints of magic in reverent ease.

Dappled Affection

Under the boughs where shadows play light,
A dance of affection feels soft and bright.
Fingers entwined, a warm, tender trace,
Heartbeats align in a quiet embrace.

Glimmers of laughter rise like the sun,
Every glance shared is a battle won.
In the dappled light, love's essence unfolds,
Holding the moments like precious gold.

The Heart's Bounty

In fields where wildflowers bloom,
The heart collects its sweet perfume.
With each petal, a whisper calls,
Tales of love that never falls.

In gentle breezes, secrets share,
Moments caught in sunlit air.
With every beat, a promise stays,
Guiding souls through winding ways.

Carnival of Thoughts

Colors dance in mind's bright fair,
Whirling dreams beyond compare.
A jester's laughter fills the sky,
Echoing where visions fly.

Cotton candy clouds declare,
Joyful wonders everywhere.
Step right up, the show begins,
In this realm, our spirit wins.

Pulse of the Night

Stars flicker on the velvet sea,
In their glow, we find the key.
Whispers float on moonlit trails,
Tales of dreams that softly sail.

Shadows breathe in silent grace,
Nature's heart, a warm embrace.
In the stillness, echoes chime,
Marking life's profoundest time.

The Warmth Between

In quiet moments, eyes align,
Words unspoken, hearts define.
A gentle touch, a knowing glance,
In this space, we find romance.

Candles flicker with soft light,
Binding two souls in the night.
Love's tender glow, a secret song,
In this warmth, we both belong.

Caress of the Breeze

Gentle whispers in the trees,
Softly dancing with the leaves.
Breezes carry tales anew,
Secrets shared between the two.

Wandering paths of sunlit gold,
A touch of warmth, a heart unfolds.
Nature's breath, a sweet embrace,
In every corner, love we trace.

Birds will sing their melodies,
Floating through the fragrant air.
Moments linger, soft and free,
A fleeting kiss beyond compare.

Underneath the cloudless skies,
Dreams arise on whispered sighs.
In the caress of the breeze,
Life finds joy with elegant ease.

An Infusion of Bliss

In morning light, the world awakes,
A tapestry of joy it makes.
Sunshine spills like golden wine,
Life's sweet moments intertwine.

With every laugh, a heart takes flight,
In simple pleasures, pure delight.
A fleeting glance, a knowing smile,
Each little spark, we cherish a while.

Sipping warmth from friendship's cup,
In shared stories, we rise up.
Laughter dances in the air,
In every bond, a love laid bare.

An infusion of bliss we find,
In gentle kisses, hearts unbind.
Through every day, may joy persist,
In every touch, a love's sweet tryst.

Fables of Enchantment

In twilight's hush, the stories weave,
Of whispered dreams that hearts believe.
Fables born of starlit nights,
Casting shadows, sparking lights.

Magic flows through every tale,
In realms where wishes never pale.
Creatures dance with grace and flair,
Guided by the dreams we share.

Through thickets deep, where echoes roam,
Adventure calls, our hearts find home.
Each fable's end, a brand new start,
We write our dreams, we play our part.

In enchanted woods, we dare to tread,
With every word, our spirits fed.
Fables of love, of hope, of cheer,
In every story, we hold dear.

Glimmers of Intrigue

In shadows cast by flickering light,
Secrets shimmer, hidden from sight.
Whispers soft, like silken threads,
Entwined in tales, where mystery spreads.

Points of sparkle in the dark,
Curiosity ignites a spark.
Every glance, a fleeting chase,
Glimmers cloak the world in grace.

With every heartbeat, tensions rise,
In uncertain paths, we seek the prize.
A dance of fate, a twirl of chance,
In every glance, the mind's romance.

The unknown calls with voices sweet,
In every riddle, intrigue's heartbeat.
With open hearts, we'll face the night,
In glimmers found, we claim our light.

Timeless Whispers

In the hush of night, secrets weave,
Echoes of dreams that hearts believe.
A gentle breeze, a soft refrain,
Whispers of love that break the chain.

Stars glimmer bright, in skies so wide,
Each twinkle a memory, love's guide.
Moonlight dances on tranquil streams,
Carrying softly our sweetest dreams.

Symphony of the Senses

Beneath the petals, scents entwine,
A melody sweet, your hand in mine.
Colors vibrant, the world unfolds,
In every moment, a story told.

Tastes of summer on our lips,
With laughter shared, a sweet eclipse.
The rhythm of life, a heart's embrace,
In this symphony, we find our place.

Flickering Glances

Across the room, our eyes collide,
In silence shared, our hearts confide.
A fleeting spark, a moment's grace,
In flickering glances, we find our space.

Time stands still, the world fades out,
In whispered breaths, there's no doubt.
With every smile, the twinkle grows,
In these stolen looks, true love flows.

Tender Interludes

In quiet corners, whispers bloom,
A soft embrace, dispelling gloom.
Gentle laughter, the warmest sighs,
In tender interludes, love never dies.

Moments linger like a sweet caress,
Each heartbeat a promise, no less.
Wrapped in warmth, our spirits fly,
In these interludes, we touch the sky.

Flickers of Passion

In the hush of night,
Whispers dance like flames,
Hearts beat in sync,
Two souls play their games.

Eyes meet in silence,
A spark ignites the dark,
Embers softly glowing,
Kindling love's sweet spark.

Moments linger softly,
Floating on warm air,
With every gentle touch,
They melt away despair.

Lost in lips' embrace,
Time ceases to exist,
In passion's sweet glow,
Two hearts can't resist.

Threads of Connection

In a world of strangers,
Threads weave in a dance,
Ties grow strong and steady,
Each glance is a chance.

Shared laughs echo brightly,
Connecting hearts anew,
In our stories woven,
Life feels warm and true.

A gentle hand offered,
In moments of doubt,
We find new beginnings,
And give love a shout.

Through trials and triumphs,
We stand side by side,
Together we flourish,
In love we abide.

Breezes of Delight

A soft wind is blowing,
Carrying sweet scents,
Nature blooms around us,
As happiness lent.

Children's laughter dances,
In the golden light,
Each moment cherished,
A pure, joyful sight.

With each gentle breeze,
We feel time slip away,
In fleeting sweetness,
We long to stay.

Even as sunlight fades,
And day greets the night,
Breezes whisper softly,
Of love's pure delight.

The Essence of Us

In quiet moments shared,
Our silence speaks so loud,
The essence of us glows,
In love, we are proud.

Through the storms we've weathered,
And the joy we have found,
Together we are stronger,
In love, we are bound.

With every kind word spoken,
We strengthen our ties,
Like stars in the heavens,
Our love never dies.

In the tapestry woven,
Of memories and trust,
We'll write our story,
In the essence of us.

Radiance of the Heart

In the quiet glow of dawn's embrace,
Whispers of love begin to trace.
Sunlight dances on gentle streams,
Filling the world with vibrant dreams.

With every beat, a story sings,
Of hidden hopes and fragile wings.
Through shadows cast, a light appears,
Unraveling all doubts and fears.

A warmth ignites, a spark divine,
Connecting souls like intertwining vine.
In this space, time softly bends,
Creating bonds that never end.

So let the heart's bright radiance show,
The depths of love, the ways it grows.
In every heartbeat, truths unfold,
A tapestry of warmth to hold.

Echoes of Intimacy

In the stillness of a shared glance,
A world unfolds in perfect dance.
Breath of whispers, soft and low,
Echoes of warmth, where shadows grow.

Two souls entwined in gentle night,
Finding comfort in the light.
Moments linger, silent charms,
Cradled softly in each other's arms.

Through hushed confessions, feelings soar,
Every heartbeat opens doors.
In the echoes of laughter shared,
The bond of love is deeply paired.

As night surrenders to dawn's sweet grace,
We treasure every fleeting space.
In intimacy, we find our song,
A melody where we belong.

Chasing the Twilight

As day retreats, the sky ignites,
With hues of amber, reds, and whites.
We chase the twilight, hand in hand,
To gather stars across the land.

The breeze carries secrets soft and low,
Whispers of night that gently flow.
Every shadow hides a dream,
As we wander where moonlight beams.

In the dance of dusk, we lose all care,
With laughter echoing in the air.
Time stands still as we explore,
The magic found in twilight's lore.

As twilight fades to starlit night,
Our hearts align, a pure delight.
In chasing moments, wild and free,
We find the depths of shared memory.

Canvas of Euphoria

Upon a canvas, colors blend,
Each brushstroke whispers, transcends.
The hues of joy, the spills of love,
Creating visions from above.

In vibrant strokes, we find our voice,
Painting dreams, we make a choice.
To fill the world with shades of grace,
A portrait blooms in time and space.

With laughter's echo and passion's fire,
We craft the scenes that won't expire.
In every curve, a story flows,
A testament of how it grows.

So let the colors fly and swirl,
In the dance of life, we twirl.
On this canvas, endless and bright,
We paint our euphoria, pure delight.

Journey Through Starlit Eyes

In the quiet night, we roam,
Beneath the vast, twinkling dome.
Each star a guide, a flickering spark,
Illuminating dreams in the dark.

With every step, the cosmos calls,
Echoes of wonder in twilight thralls.
Footprints on the path of the divine,
In starlit eyes, our fates entwine.

Through whispers of the astral breeze,
We dance beneath the ancient trees.
The universe hums a timeless tune,
As we sail on the wings of the moon.

Our journey flows like a river of light,
Shimmering softly in the gentle night.
With starlit eyes, the world feels new,
In a tapestry woven from dreams come true.

Whispers of Emotion

In shadows cast by fading light,
Emotions flicker, soft and bright.
With every whisper, hearts collide,
A symphony where truths reside.

In tender moments, feelings swell,
Stories from the soul we tell.
Through laughter bright and sorrow deep,
A dance of dreams, a chance to leap.

The silence speaks, yet voices soar,
In every glance, we long for more.
With open hearts, we learn to feel,
The gentle power of what's real.

Emotions wade like rivers wide,
Carving paths where love can glide.
In whispered tones, our spirits rise,
Together we weave the seen and the wise.

A Dance of Shadows

In twilight's embrace, shadows sway,
Mingling softly at end of day.
With every move, a tale untold,
In the dance of night, the world unfolds.

The flicker of light meets darkest hue,
A duet where fears are drawn anew.
Spirits twirl in the whispering breeze,
Lost in the moment, hearts feel at ease.

With shadows cast, we feel alive,
In this dance where memories thrive.
Each step a story, a fleeting spark,
In the gentle night, we leave our mark.

Through the rhythm of the shifting shade,
We find our path, unafraid.
In the dance of shadows, souls unite,
In softest whispers, we take flight.

Serenade of the Heart

In the still of night, sweet melodies flow,
A serenade soft, where true feelings grow.
Each note a whisper, a promise so bright,
Wrapped in the warmth of love's gentle light.

With every heartbeat, the music unfolds,
Tales of affection that history holds.
A symphony swells in the quiet of dreams,
Awakening passion as starlight gleams.

Guitar strings cry in the moon's soft glow,
Every strum carries the stories we know.
The serenade dances through shadow and spark,
Uniting our souls, igniting the dark.

In harmony's embrace, we find our way,
Through the serenade, night turns to day.
With hearts wide open, we sing our part,
In the melody woven, a love-filled heart.

Serenade at Dusk

Whispers of night fall, soft and low,
As shadows stretch and the stars start to glow.
A melody dances on the cool evening air,
While crickets join in with their gentle care.

The moon begins rising, silver and bright,
Casting its glow, a serene, lovely sight.
With every soft note, hearts begin to sway,
In this tender moment, as night turns to play.

Flames of Anticipation

In the crackling fire, sparks take to flight,
Dreams are ignited, flickering bright.
With eyes wide open, we gaze at the flame,
Every heartbeat whispers, never the same.

The warmth wraps around us, like a sweet embrace,
A dance of emotions in this sacred space.
We breathe in the moments, feeling alive,
In the flames of anticipation, we thrive.

Heartbeats in Harmony

Two souls intertwined, beating as one,
In sync with the rhythms, our journey begun.
With every soft glance, our pulses align,
A symphony sweet, your heart next to mine.

The world fades away, just a whispering tune,
Under the stars, beneath the bright moon.
We dance through the evening, lost in the sway,
Heartbeats in harmony, come what may.

Reflections of Bliss

In the stillness of morning, with dew on the grass,
The sunlight breaks softly, the moments pass.
Each glimmer a promise of joy to unfold,
In reflections of bliss, we find treasures untold.

As laughter surrounds us, a warm, friendly sound,
In echoes of happiness, peace can be found.
With every bright sunrise, a chance to embrace,
The beauty of living, this wondrous place.

The Dance of Affection

In the moonlight's gentle glow,
Hearts entwined, love starts to flow.
Every glance, a soft embrace,
Two souls find their sacred space.

Whispers sweet, secrets shared,
In that moment, all is bared.
Feet move as if in a trance,
Life's a rhythm, love's the dance.

With every twirl, the world fades,
In warmth of touch, affection wades.
Eyes that speak, words left unsaid,
A language deep, where love is fed.

As stars align, the night stands still,
In this dance, hearts feel the thrill.
Together, we write our song,
In the dance of love, we belong.

Waves of Yearning

Upon the shore, the tides do call,
Yearning hearts, we rise and fall.
Each wave whispers secrets deep,
In the silence, love we keep.

The ocean's breath, a longing sigh,
As stars above light the sky.
With every crash, a dream takes flight,
In the dark, we find our light.

Salt-kissed air, the moonlight's glow,
Guiding paths where lovers go.
In the depths, our hopes reside,
As the waves become our guide.

From shore to shore, we chase the tide,
In the currents, hearts collide.
Forever drawn, we can't resist,
In the waves, love's gentle tryst.

Veils of Serenity

In gardens where the flowers bloom,
Peaceful hearts can find their room.
Veils of green, the softest shade,
In this calm, our fears all fade.

Whispered winds, they gently sway,
Bringing warmth to light the way.
Butterflies dance, a fleeting sigh,
In the hush, dreams float by.

Serene waters, a crystal lake,
Mirroring wishes that we make.
In the stillness, time stands still,
Holding close, what hearts can feel.

With every breath, the world's at ease,
Nature's song brings gentle peace.
Wrapped in love, we find our way,
In the veils where calm will stay.

The Tapestry of Dreams

Threads of gold in the night sky,
Weaving tales where hopes can fly.
Each dream stitched with care and grace,
In this tapestry, we find our place.

Laughter bright as colors blend,
In this art, our souls transcend.
Whispers float on the evening air,
Binding hearts with love and care.

Across the loom, visions unfold,
Stories of hearts, both brave and bold.
With every thread, a journey starts,
In the weave, we share our hearts.

When morning light begins to break,
In our dreams, a path we make.
Forever drawn to this grand scheme,
Together we'll chase every dream.

Moments in Reverie

In whispered dreams, the shadows dance,
A fleeting glimpse, a longing glance.
Soft petals fall, like thoughts in flight,
Holding silence tight, through the night.

Memories sway, like trees in spring,
Echoes of laughter, the heart does sing.
Time weaves moments, a delicate thread,
With every heartbeat, the past is fed.

Caress of Time

Time flows gently, like a river wide,
Each tick a whisper, a moment's guide.
Golden rays brush the world anew,
Caressing life with a tender hue.

Ticking clocks hum a soothing sound,
In their embrace, lost dreams are found.
Each second a gem, each hour a song,
In the caress of time, where we belong.

The Alchemy of Feeling

In the depths of hearts, a spark ignites,
Transforming silence into vibrant sights.
Alchemy blooms in the realm of dreams,
Where nothing's ever quite what it seems.

Emotions blend, like colors on a muse,
Painting the canvas, we cannot refuse.
Each heartbeat a chance, each sigh a start,
The alchemy of feeling, a work of art.

Enchantment of the Instant

In a heartbeat, magic comes alive,
Moments shimmer, as dreams arrive.
The instant whispers secrets untold,
In brief encounters, our hearts behold.

A glance exchanged, a smile so bright,
Enchantment blooms in the soft twilight.
Each second a treasure, a fleeting kiss,
In the enchantment of the instant, we find bliss.

Awakening the Undercurrent

In shadows deep where silence breathes,
A whisper stirs the dormancy.
Beneath the waves of quiet dreams,
The current flows with energy.

It dances low, a subtle spark,
In realms untouched by light of day.
Awakening the hidden arc,
It pulls the heart, it guides the sway.

A symphony of hidden tides,
Unseen forces at play within.
With every rise, the spirit glides,
And fears dissolve as dawn begins.

The world emerges, bright and clear,
As dreams unfold and laughter springs.
Awakening the soul's frontier,
In every breath, the promise sings.

Silent Ballet

In the hush of velvet night,
Moonlight drapes a gentle cloak.
Stars align in quiet flight,
Whispers dance, and silence spoke.

A pirouette of silver beams,
Every twirl a soft embrace.
Through the stillness, truth redeems,
In shadows, we find our grace.

Choreographed by unseen hands,
Every heartbeat marks a turn.
The soul's rhythm understands,
In the still, our spirits yearn.

This ballet sung without a sound,
Echoes felt but never shown.
Together lost, together found,
In twilight's art, we are not alone.

A Fusion of Wonder

In colors bright that blend and swirl,
Imagination paints the skies.
A fusion of beauty starts to unfurl,
As dreams awaken, hope will rise.

The stars align in cosmic play,
Galaxies whisper secrets slight.
Each moment shines, a brand new day,
Where every heart begins its flight.

Through trees of gold and azure seas,
Wonders weave a tapestry.
In every leaf, a gentle breeze,
In each caress, we find the key.

Celebrate the song of life,
In every heartbeat, every glance.
A fusion that transcends all strife,
In awe we breathe, in love we dance.

Veins of Bliss

Through quiet woods where secrets lie,
A pulse of joy runs deep and clear.
Each step unveils the whispered sigh,
In nature's heart, we lose our fear.

Veins of bliss flow soft and free,
In every leaf, in every stream.
The world embraces harmony,
A tapestry of love and dream.

Rivers dance with laughter bright,
While flowers bloom in vibrant hue.
In every breath, the purest light,
Brings forth the soul, renews the view.

In moments held, we come alive,
The essence of what truly is.
With every heartbeat, we arrive,
In sacred space, we find our bliss.

Breath of Longing

In the quiet of the night,
Whispers of the heart take flight.
Stars gleam with a softer glow,
Yearning for the dreams we sow.

A gentle sigh escapes the lips,
As hope from the soul gently drips.
Fingers trace a distant line,
Touching shadows where you shine.

Candles flicker, shadows dance,
In the silence, we find our chance.
To hold the moments in between,
Where love's echoes can be seen.

With every breath, a promise made,
In longing's arms, we are laid.
Together, we will find the way,
In the dawn of a brand new day.

Sunlight Through the Veil

Morning rays break the night,
Softening the world's delight.
Veils of mist begin to part,
Letting warmth into the heart.

Glistening dew on petals bright,
Whispers of a pure delight.
Each beam a sweet caress,
Bringing forth nature's dress.

Trees sway in the gentle breeze,
Their leaves dance with graceful ease.
Golden light spills like honey,
Filling spaces bright and funny.

As shadows melt beneath the sun,
In this moment, we are one.
Basking in the warm embrace,
Of sunlight's soft-held grace.

A Symphony of Feelings

In the stillness, music plays,
Echoing through endless days.
Notes of joy and sorrow blend,
In a melody that won't end.

Hearts beat to a rhythmic tune,
Chasing dreams beneath the moon.
Each emotion finds its place,
In the symphony of grace.

Love's refrain, sweet and strong,
Carries us where we belong.
A dance of souls, a gentle sway,
In the harmony of play.

As hearts unite, a chorus grows,
Flooding us with all that glows.
In every measure, life reveals,
The beauty of our diverse feels.

Gossamer Dreams

In a world where thoughts take flight,
Delicate as the dawn's first light.
We weave our dreams on silver seams,
Holding fast the gossamer beams.

Fragile visions whisper low,
In twilight's gentle, tender flow.
Each wish a petal on the breeze,
Carried far with graceful ease.

Shapes of hope in shadows cast,
Through the fabric of the past.
Bridges built from heart to heart,
Where every dream may find its start.

As the night fades into day,
We chase the whispers, come what may.
In gossamer dreams, we believe,
In every promise we receive.

Transcendental Reflections

In stillness found, we gaze above,
The cosmos whispers tales of love.
Stars align in a silent dance,
We drift together, lost in trance.

Echoes of dreams in twilight's hue,
Fleeting glimpses of worlds anew.
Time unwinds, a gentle stream,
Life unfolds, a boundless dream.

Mountains rise, and rivers flow,
Nature's pulse, a sacred glow.
Wisdom rests in every sigh,
Beneath the vast and open sky.

Between the lines of heart and mind,
Transcendent truths are there to find.
In every breath, a chance to see,
The universe inside of me.

Spellbound Moments

In fleeting time, we find our place,
Each heartbeat shares a tender grace.
The world ignites in colors rare,
As laughter dances through the air.

Caught in the glow of summer's light,
We chase the dusk and hold on tight.
Every smile a magic spell,
In secret spaces, stories dwell.

Whispers soft beneath the moon,
Together as the stars attune.
Each second stretched, a treasure chest,
In spellbound moments, we are blessed.

Time can pause in love's embrace,
Memories etched in this sacred space.
With open hearts, we learn to feel,
The fleeting wish of dreams made real.

Eclipsed by Emotion

In shadows cast by heart's delight,
We lose ourselves in the night.
Whispers cloud the silken air,
Eclipsed by moments laid so bare.

Every tear, a story untold,
In silence, our secrets unfold.
Like tides that rise and fall away,
Emotions dance, a wild ballet.

The light may dim, but hearts ignite,
In darkness, we find our light.
Through storms that rage and moments meek,
We seek the solace that we speak.

Together we embrace the sway,
In shadows cast, come what may.
Eclipsed by emotions that entwine,
In vulnerability, we shine.

The Language of Ripples

In still waters, whispers twine,
The language of ripples, soft and fine.
Each touch upon the surface clear,
Unfolds the tales that draw us near.

Gentle waves speak of the past,
In their rhythm, memories cast.
The flow of time, a soothing balm,
In nature's song, we find our calm.

Beneath the surface, currents sway,
We navigate the light of day.
With every ripple, hearts are shared,
A dance of feelings long declared.

In quiet moments, wisdom flows,
The language of ripples softly shows.
In the embrace of liquid sighs,
We find the truths that never die.

The Spirit's Palette

Colors dance upon the breeze,
Whispers of the heart's desires.
In every hue, a story flows,
A canvas bright, where spirit soars.

Brush of joy, stroke of pain,
Life's great art, a wild refrain.
With every shade, a note we sing,
In this gallery, our souls take wing.

Through the spectrum, we discover,
Wisdom wrapped in every color.
Each stroke tells of love and loss,
In this masterpiece, we find our gloss.

In the silence, beauty speaks,
In the shadows, light unique.
Together woven, shadows blend,
The spirit's palette never ends.

Vibrations of the Soul

Echoes linger in the night,
Melodies that spark the light.
In each heartbeat, a silent tune,
Vibration whispers to the moon.

Through the dark, the rhythms play,
Guiding dreams that drift away.
In the stillness, voices call,
To awaken the heart in all.

Dance of stars, pulse of time,
Symphony in every rhyme.
From deep within, our spirits rise,
In harmony, the universe replies.

Feel the waves that softly sway,
In each moment, find your way.
Connected in this sacred role,
We are one, vibrations of the soul.

Lure of the Luminous

Stars aglow in velvet night,
Hearts are drawn to their soft light.
With a whisper, they ignite,
Dreams of wonder take to flight.

In the shadows, sparks arise,
Guiding seekers with their eyes.
A dance of hope that shines so bright,
Connecting worlds beyond our sight.

Radiance calls with gentle grace,
Illuminating every space.
Like a moth drawn to the flame,
We are changed, but not the same.

Toward the glow, our spirits yearn,
In each flicker, lessons learned.
In the night, we find our way,
Lure of the luminous, night and day.

When Stars Align

In the cosmos, fates intertwine,
Moments spark when stars align.
Paths collide in perfect grace,
Creating magic in this space.

Time stands still, the world awakes,
Synchronicity its gift makes.
In the dance of love, we find,
The universe is truly kind.

Gentle tides, a cosmic flow,
In destined hearts, a seed will grow.
Every wish and breath combined,
Create the wonders we designed.

In this glimpse of fate's embrace,
We cherish life, its sweetened taste.
When the stars align, so true,
Boundless dreams, forever new.

Secrets in the Air

Whispers drift on evening's breath,
Floating softly, life and death.
Mysteries linger through the trees,
Carried gently by the breeze.

Hidden truths that softly sigh,
Caught between the stars and sky.
In the silence, secrets dwell,
Echoes of a distant spell.

Voices weave through twilight's veil,
Softly telling ancient tales.
Each one vibrant, each one rare,
Forever living in the air.

So listen close, the night is deep,
In the shadows, secrets keep.
Nighttime's gift, both bold and fair,
Lies revealed in dreams we share.

Intricate Tangles

Threads of life, twisted and spun,
Knots that form as daylight's done.
Connections made through joy and pain,
In this dance, we break the chain.

We find ourselves in every thread,
Woven tales where paths have led.
Through the tangle, hearts entwine,
In the chaos, love will shine.

Every twist a story told,
In each fiber, memories hold.
Crafting bonds that time won't sever,
Intricate, yet light as ever.

Through the maze of human fate,
Together, we appreciate.
In tangled webs, strong we stand,
A tapestry hand in hand.

Flavors of the Night

Moonlight spills on velvet skies,
Sweet as dreams that gently rise.
A sip of stars, a dash of night,
Stirring shadows, pure delight.

Whispers dance in cool, fresh air,
Savory scents from everywhere.
The taste of mystery unfolds,
In silent tales that darkness holds.

Flavors rich, both wild and sweet,
Decked in starlight, a rare treat.
Beneath the warmth of evening glow,
Every heart begins to flow.

Sip the night, let senses soar,
Find the magic at its core.
In each moment, pure and bright,
Life reveals its flavors right.

Wistful Daydreams

In the quiet of the morn,
Thoughts take flight, a world reborn.
Memories drift like clouds above,
Soft reflections of lost love.

Wistful dreams that gently play,
Paint the skies in shades of grey.
Chasing moments not yet seized,
In the heart, a longing pleased.

Time suspended in sweet delight,
Hours stretch to hold the night.
Every whisper, every sigh,
Tells a story that won't die.

Embrace the fleeting, hold it near,
Breathe in hope, diminish fear.
In daydreams' arms, we softly sleep,
Finding solace, secrets keep.

Shadows of Serenity

In twilight's gentle embrace,
Whispers of peace take flight.
Moonlight dances on the lake,
While stars hold secrets tight.

Breezes carry softest sighs,
Among the willows tall.
Shadows weave through tranquil dreams,
As night begins to fall.

Reflections spark a quiet hope,
Calm waters mirror the sky.
In this moment, hearts can rest,
And let their worries fly.

Embraced by dusk's warm glow,
Each breath a soothing balm.
In shadows, peace awakens,
And fills the world with calm.

Awakened Passions

In the dance of morning light,
Hearts ignite with fierce desire.
Raindrops fall like whispered dreams,
Setting souls and thoughts afire.

Fingers brush, electric sparks,
As melodies intertwine.
With every glance and fleeting touch,
The world fades into time.

Rhythms pulse, a sacred beat,
A chant that stirs the heart.
Awakened passions flare anew,
Each moment a fresh start.

Together lost in fervent waves,
No boundaries left to see.
In this dance of raw emotion,
We find our true decree.

Tender Vibes

In soft light of a fading day,
Tender vibes begin to flow.
Laughter dances on the breeze,
As time slows down, we glow.

Quiet moments, shared with love,
Eyes that speak without a sound.
In each heartbeat, warmth unfolds,
A place where hope is found.

The world outside fades away,
As we create our space.
Every touch, a gentle song,
In a sweet, endearing grace.

Held in dreams, in every sigh,
We weave our spirits tight.
In tender vibes, we just exist,
Two souls in pure delight.

The Pulse of Silence

In the hush of twilight's glow,
A pulse begins to resonate.
Each heartbeat, a soft echo,
Whispers of the world await.

Branches sway in gentle sighs,
Nature holds its breath in awe.
In this space, we find a truth,
A beauty we can draw.

Between the beats, a vast expanse,
Where thoughts become the light.
In silence, dreams begin to bloom,
Unfurled by stars so bright.

The pulse of silence speaks so loud,
In stillness, we take flight.
A journey on the wings of night,
Into the heart of light.

The Flicker of Desire

In twilight's gentle glow, we meet,
A spark ignites, a heart's quick beat.
Whispers dance upon the air,
Cloaked in dreams, we find our stare.

A candle's flame, it flickers bright,
A tender touch in fading light.
With every glance, the passion grows,
In silent night, our longing flows.

Secrets shared beneath the stars,
As night unveils our hidden scars.
Like moths we flutter, drawn to fire,
In the shadows, the flicker of desire.

Together lost, yet found in bliss,
Each moment cherished, sealed with a kiss.
The world outside begins to blur,
Two souls entwined in sweet demur.

Tides of Yearning

The ocean calls with rhythmic sighs,
Waves crashing soft beneath the skies.
My heart, it drifts on currents wide,
In the embrace of the restless tide.

With every wave, a whispered plea,
For distant shores where I long to be.
The moonlit path, it guides me there,
To lands where love hangs in the air.

In depths so deep, my spirit swims,
Searching for light at the ocean's rims.
Each pulse of water stirs my soul,
A dance of yearning, forever whole.

As tides recede, I feel the pull,
Of memories that keep me full.
The ache remains, a trusted friend,
Until the waves bring you again.

Chasing Fancies

In a world where wishes fly,
Dreams take shape beneath the sky.
We chase the stars that glitter bright,
With hearts aligned, we soar in flight.

Each fancy spins a tale anew,
Of distant lands and skies so blue.
With every step, we leave a trace,
In the garden of time, we find our place.

The laughter echoes, pure delight,
As shadows fade with the coming light.
In every moment, magic sparks,
In chasing fancies, we leave our marks.

The journey beckons, calling loud,
Each day a canvas, vibrant, proud.
Together we weave our dreams in threads,
In this dance of life, where fantasy spreads.

Echoes of Elation

In the heart of joy, we find our tune,
A melody bright, under the moon.
Laughter lingers in the air,
Each note a treasure, pure and rare.

With every heartbeat, we partake,
The echoes rise, a joyful wake.
Moments shared, like starlit skies,
Illuminate the wonder in our eyes.

In the rush of life, our spirits soar,
Dancing through the open door.
We celebrate the love we share,
A symphony, beyond compare.

As we journey through each bright day,
The echoes of elation lead the way.
Together we sing, our spirits free,
In harmony's embrace, you and me.

Glowing Desire

In the moonlight's gentle gaze,
Whispers stir the silent night.
Hearts aflame in passion's haze,
Lost in dreams, their souls take flight.

Fingers trace a tender path,
With each touch, a spark ignites.
Sparks of laughter, gentle wrath,
In the dark, their love unites.

Time stands still, the world fades away,
Only they, in glowing fire.
Wrapped in warmth, they dare to sway,
Endless love, their heart's desire.

Stars above witness the dance,
Of two souls in radiant bloom.
In each glance, a fateful chance,
A glowing love, dispelling gloom.

Morning's Dance

Sunlight breaks the night's embrace,
Birds awaken, greet the dawn.
Nature stirs with gentle grace,
As the weary night is gone.

Petals open, colors bright,
Dewdrops glisten, diamonds near.
Each moment feels so right,
Morning's dance now draws us near.

Whispers of the breeze, so sweet,
Rustling leaves in soft refrain.
Life's rhythm, a joyful beat,
In this calm, all worries wane.

As the sun climbs to the sky,
Shadows fade, the world awakes.
In the light, dreams learn to fly,
Morning's dance, a love that makes.

A Canvas of Hues

Brushstrokes blend, a life portrayed,
Colors mingling, heart's delight.
In each shade, a memory laid,
A canvas breathes, alive and bright.

Crimson whispers tales of love,
Azure dreams and hopes unfurled.
Golden suns and skies above,
Craft a tapestry of the world.

Each hue speaks of moments lost,
Of laughter shared and tears they cried.
Art reflects the dreams we cost,
And in its depths, our souls reside.

As colors dance upon the page,
Life's stories flow in vibrant streams.
With every stroke, we set the stage,
A canvas filled with vivid dreams.

Harmonies of the Heart

Notes unfold like petals fair,
Melodies that intertwine.
In the air, love's sweetened flare,
Each heartbeat marks its perfect line.

Rhythms rise, a gentle tune,
Bringing souls in close embrace.
Underneath the silver moon,
Every glance, a warm caress.

Chords resound, emotions swell,
With each breath, the music grows.
In this space, they know it well,
Harmony that softly flows.

Together, they compose the song,
A symphony that knows no end.
Through life's journey, they belong,
Harmonies that fate would send.

A Tapestry of Whispers

In shadows soft and dim, it weaves,
Threads of secrets in the eaves.
Silence dances, a gentle sway,
Softly urging night to stay.

Nature speaks in hushed tones low,
Revealing truths that only grow.
Whispers travel on the breeze,
Carrying dreams through swaying trees.

Each word a stitch, each sigh a seam,
Crafting moments, weaving dreams.
Entwined souls in the quiet dark,
Kindling soft, a tender spark.

A tapestry spun from heart's own thread,
In every whisper, love is wed.
Listen closely, feel the blend,
In every murmur, hearts transcend.

Elixirs of Ecstasy

In twilight's glow, they shimmer bright,
Bottled dreams, pure delight.
Sipping joy from crystal glass,
Moments fleeting, forever pass.

A dash of laughter, a pinch of grace,
Each elixir finds its place.
Chasing stars with every taste,
Life's sweet nectar, never waste.

In every drop, the world ignites,
Fleeting passions, endless heights.
Stirring hearts, a vibrant blend,
With every sip, our spirits mend.

Elixirs crafted in sunset's hue,
Mirrored dreams, both old and new.
Raise your glass to the skies above,
To life, to laughter, to endless love.

The Art of Invitation

A gentle nod, a welcoming smile,
Come join me for a little while.
In gestures small, the heart expands,
Weave connection with open hands.

Through doors ajar, the laughter flows,
Inviting warmth where friendship grows.
A table set for tales to share,
In every moment, the love laid bare.

The art of gathering hearts at play,
In simple ways that light the day.
Take a step, let spirits soar,
For in this dance, we find our core.

An open heart, a space to be,
In invitation, we are free.
Together weaving life's great song,
In unity where we belong.

Chimes of Connection

In the quiet, chimes resound,
Echoes of love, unbound.
Each note a bridge to another's heart,
In harmony, we play our part.

With every ring, a story told,
Memories cherished, fading bold.
Whispers carried on the wind,
In this dance, we are twinned.

Connection flows like rivers wide,
Uniting souls in ebb and tide.
To listen close is to feel the spark,
Of bonds that shine within the dark.

Chimes of joy in the open air,
Resonate with love and care.
Join the rhythm, let it sing,
In every heart, let chimes take wing.

heartbeat of the Universe

In the vast expanse, stars align,
A pulse beats softly, so divine.
Galaxies dance in swirling light,
Whispers of time in the quiet night.

Each moment echoes, eternally true,
A symphony crafted for me and you.
Gravity pulls, as love finds its way,
In the heartbeat of night, in the dawn's first ray.

Cosmic tides swell, then drift apart,
Yet, within this chaos, we feel the heart.
Every twinkle, a never-ending sigh,
In the universe's pulse, we learn to fly.

Together we sway, lost in the dance,
Life's rhythms expressed in glances.
As we orbit through joy and strife,
Feel the heartbeat—it's a song of life.

The Alchemy of Desire

In the furnace of dreams, passions ignite,
Transforming the mundane into shimmering light.
A flicker of hope, a whisper of grace,
Desire's elixir, in time and space.

Sifting through shadows, we seek what is real,
The magic of longing, a potent appeal.
Craving the unknown, we reach and we strive,
In the alchemy of yearning, we come alive.

With every heartbeat, every breath we take,
The essence of longing, the choices we make.
Transformative power in each soul's fire,
We dance through the ages: desire, aspire.

In the crucible's heat, friendships grow strong,
In loving connections, we find where we belong.
The alchemy of desire, a force so grand,
Unleashing our spirits, hand in hand.

Reverberations of Joy

From laughter's spark, a ripple ignites,
Joy blossoms forth, painting our sights.
A melody hums in the hearts of kin,
Reverberations echo, pulling us in.

In moments of kindness, in gentle embrace,
Joy multiplies, it fills every space.
With every shared glance, with every soft sigh,
We weave together, as time flutters by.

Like sunlight's kiss on the morning dew,
Laughter unfolds, warm and true.
Chasing our shadows, we dance on the waves,
In the reverberations, love's spirit saves.

In whispers and shouts, in waves of pure light,
Joy wraps around us, holding us tight.
Together we stand, together we sing,
In the symphony of life, oh, what joy it brings!

An Ode to Whimsy

In the garden of dreams, where wonders sprout,
Whimsy is dancing, without a doubt.
With colors that twirl and stories that spin,
An ode to imagination, let the fun begin.

The moon wears a hat, the sun paints a grin,
In this playful realm, we're all invited in.
Where the clouds are made of cotton candy fluff,
And every adventure says, 'You've had enough!'

Fairies and giants, a curious blend,
In the land of whimsy, rules break and bend.
We ride on the back of a silver-winged dream,
Life is a canvas; let your heart beam.

So lift up your spirits, let your laughter flow,
For whimsy's a treasure we all need to know.
In this joyful dance, let your heart take flight,
An ode to whimsy, a world of delight.

Craving the Night

The moon hangs low in the sky,
Whispers of dreams softly sigh.
Stars flicker like distant fireflies,
In shadows, our secret lies.

A blanket of velvet above,
Where silence cradles the world we love.
Each heartbeat echoes through the dark,
In the night, we find our spark.

We chase the breeze on midnight's wing,
Dancing with shadows, our spirits sing.
With every breath, the night feels right,
In this embrace, we crave the night.

Time stands still in the moon's embrace,
Lost in the magic of this sacred space.
With every glance, our souls ignite,
Together, we dwell in the endless night.

Blossoms of Sentiment

In the garden of thoughts, love blooms,
Whispers of joy amid the glooms.
Each petal unfurls with memories sweet,
In the heart's embrace, our souls meet.

Sunlight drips through the leaves above,
Painting the landscape with colors of love.
Fragrant breezes caress the air,
In this serene moment, we share.

Time flows gently like a stream,
In this meadow, we weave our dream.
With every blossom, a story told,
In the fabric of sentiment, we unfold.

Amidst the petals, laughter rings,
Echoes of life, the joy it brings.
In the shadows, our hopes take flight,
Blossoms of sentiment, pure and bright.

The Language of Silence

In quiet moments, whispers reside,
A symphony where thoughts collide.
The unspoken words float in the air,
In the silence, we find what we share.

Eyes convey what lips cannot say,
In the stillness, we drift away.
Every heartbeat, a gentle sound,
In this silence, love is found.

The world fades softly, shadows blend,
In this space, we transcend.
A language deeper than words could tell,
In our silence, all is well.

As stars draw closer and time unwinds,
In the hush, our hearts entwined.
The language of silence, rare and divine,
In this moment, your soul meets mine.

Embrace of the Stars

Under the heavens, our dreams collide,
In the stillness, where secrets hide.
Stars twinkle like diamonds above,
In this vast sky, we feel the love.

Hands held tight in the cool night air,
Mapping constellations, our hearts laid bare.
Every wish cast into the night,
In the embrace, everything feels right.

The cosmos hums a gentle tune,
Under the watchful gaze of the moon.
In this embrace of endless light,
We dance softly through the night.

As galaxies swirl and comets fly,
We lose ourselves in the night sky.
In the embrace of the stars so bright,
We find our way, we find our light.

Moments of Crescendo

In whispers soft, the night unfolds,
A symphony of dreams retold.
The heart beats loud, a rhythm true,
As stars above ignite the blue.

Emotions swell, a tidal wave,
Each note we cherish, each moment brave.
With every breath, the music sways,
In crescendo, love's sweet blaze.

The world dissolves in notes divine,
Together, hearts in perfect line.
With passion's fire, we intertwine,
In moments seized, your hand in mine.

Through every sigh, the echoes soar,
In symphonies, we find our core.
Let time suspend, this night, our stage,
In moments bright, we dance, we rage.

Hidden Affections

In shadows deep, love's whispers play,
A tender glance, we hide away.
With secret smiles, our hearts align,
In silent words, the stars combine.

A fleeting touch, electric fire,
From quiet depths, we both conspire.
In stolen moments, our hearts race,
Each hidden glance, a soft embrace.

The world outside, a distant hum,
While in this space, our hearts succumb.
With every laugh, unspoken joy,
In hidden paths, love's purest ploy.

So let us weave this secret thread,
With all that's said, and all that's fled.
In hidden affections, truth will rise,
Our love, a treasure in disguise.

Radiance of Rapture

With morning light, the earth ignites,
In colors bright, our spirit flights.
Each blossom blooms, a sweet refrain,
In nature's arms, we lose the pain.

The sunbeams dance on dewdrop's face,
In every glow, a warm embrace.
With laughter's sound, the heart expands,
As joy cascades through golden sands.

In radiant hues, our love shines clear,
A tapestry of dreams held near.
With every pulse, this rapture grows,
In open fields where wildflowers pose.

So let us bask, in love's embrace,
In beauty found, in common grace.
With every moment, we align,
In radiance, your heart with mine.

Swaying in Stillness

In quietude, we find our beat,
As stillness wraps our hearts in heat.
With gentle breaths, our souls entwine,
In swirling peace, your hand in mine.

The world outside, a distant call,
As we remain, we risk it all.
In tranquil moments, time stands still,
Where every glance ignites the thrill.

With whispered words, we weave the air,
In tender hearts, a dance we share.
With every sigh, the silence speaks,
In swaying warmth, the solace peaks.

So here we stand, in love's embrace,
Swaying softly, in our own space.
With every heartbeat, the stillness sings,
In moments pure, our spirit clings.

Whispers of Desire

In the twilight, softly we meet,
A glance shared, our hearts skip a beat.
Breathless whispers, secrets unfold,
Desires ignited, stories untold.

Under the stars, we linger near,
In silence, your voice is all I hear.
The warmth of your hand ignites the night,
A dance of shadows, love's pure light.

Moments pass, yet never fade,
In whispers of desire, bonds are laid.
A fleeting touch, a lingering sigh,
In this hush, together we fly.

With every heartbeat, passion grows strong,
In the melody of us, we belong.
Through this night, let dreams inspire,
In the darkness, we chase our fire.

A Symphony of Feelings

Notes of laughter float through the air,
Every glance a silent prayer.
Echoes of joy, rising like smoke,
In this symphony, hearts intertwine folk.

Strings of sorrow, softly weep,
In harmony, the secrets we keep.
Melodies dance, painting our fate,
The rhythm of life, we create.

Chords of longing strike a pure chord,
Together, in silence, our spirits soared.
Waves of emotion crash and swell,
In each heartbeat, a story to tell.

A ballad of dreams in the night,
With every pulse, we take flight.
Together we compose, hand in hand,
In the symphony of us, we stand.

Shadows of Longing

In the corner, shadows creep,
Filling the space, secrets to keep.
Each fading light reveals the truth,
In the silence, echoes of youth.

A heart that aches for what's out of reach,
Lessons of love, the pain they teach.
Memories linger like a soft breeze,
In the shadows, desires tease.

The moonlight whispers tales untold,
In the darkness, our dreams unfold.
With every heartbeat, time stands still,
In the shadow's embrace, we find our will.

Together we wander through the night,
Searching for hope, for love, for light.
In the stillness, a promise formed,
Through shadows of longing, we are warmed.

The Pulse of Emotion

A heartbeat quickens, the night is alive,
In the chaos of feelings, we thrive.
The pulse of passion, strong and fierce,
In gentle moments, our souls pierce.

With every glance, a story ignites,
In the rhythm of love, our spirits take flight.
Waves crash gently against the shore,
With each touch, we crave for more.

The softest whispers hum through the air,
In the cacophony of life, we dare.
Through laughter, through tears, we flow,
In the pulse of emotion, we grow.

Together we stand, hand in hand,
In the heartbeat of dreams, we understand.
United in passion, we rise and fall,
In this symphony of love, we hear the call.

Moonlit Reveries

In the hush of night, dreams arise,
Bathed in silver light, under starlit skies.
Whispers of shadows dance and twirl,
Echoes of wonders in this tranquil whirl.

Softly they call, these visions bright,
Guiding our thoughts with gentle delight.
Moonbeams weave tales of the heart,
In this quiet magic, we play our part.

Each moment a treasure, a fleeting glance,
Inviting our souls to join in the dance.
Lost in the beauty, we drift and glide,
Wrapped in the moon's glowing, tender tide.

Awake in the dreams, we find our way,
Under the watch of night's soft sway.
A realm of reveries, woven tight,
Embracing the wonders of the night.

Veils of Intimacy

In quiet corners, hearts entwined,
Soft whispers linger, secrets defined.
Veils of intimacy, gentle and near,
Echoes of laughter, a soft, sweet cheer.

Moments of silence speak volumes loud,
Wrapped in each other, lost in the crowd.
Eyes that glimmer with stories untold,
Fragile connections, both warm and bold.

Fingers entwining like vines on a wall,
In the dance of shadows, we rise and fall.
Every glance shared, a promise, a thread,
In the tapestry woven, love softly spread.

With the night deepening, we linger more,
In the still of the hours, our spirits soar.
Veils part and flutter, revealing the light,
In this sacred space, our souls unite.

Revelry of Colors

In a burst of hues, the world awakes,
Painted horizons, a canvas that breaks.
Crimson and gold dance in the sky,
Each shade a whisper, a joyful sigh.

Fields of wildflowers, a vibrant display,
Nature rejoices in colorful array.
Brushstrokes of joy across the green land,
A festival of color, so blissfully grand.

Beneath the bright arcs of the setting sun,
Life's vivid moments, a day just begun.
Each color a heartbeat, each tone a thrill,
In the revelry of life, our spirits spill.

As twilight descends, colors blend and fade,
Memories linger, in brilliance laid.
In the play of shadows, new shades we find,
A celebration of beauty, forever entwined.

The Call of Dusk

As daylight dwindles, a soft embrace,
The call of dusk in this serene space.
Stars begin to blink, shyly they peep,
In the tranquil twilight, the world sinks deep.

Whispers of evening float on the breeze,
Wrapping the night in a gentle tease.
Silhouettes stretch long in fading light,
Embracing the calm that follows the fight.

Mysterious shadows gather and sway,
Crickets serenade the close of day.
With twilight's painting, the sky blurs and bends,
In the arms of dusk, every journey transcends.

Then softly, a hush, as the stars align,
The call of the night, a beautiful sign.
In the heart of dusk, we find our peace,
As the world whispers secrets, our worries cease.

Dreamscapes of Affection

In twilight hues, our hearts align,
Beneath the stars, your hand in mine.
We wander through the night's sweet veil,
In dreamscapes where our whispers sail.

Soft laughter dances on the breeze,
Timezone slips, time's sweet tease.
Moments linger, soft and bright,
United in a world of light.

Through silver skies, our wishes fly,
Carving paths where lovers sigh.
Each heartbeat echoes in the dark,
Love's own map, a guiding spark.

In this realm, no fear resides,
With every breath, our passion glides.
Held in the warmth of dreams unspoken,
In affection's arms, we're gently woven.

Timid Flames

A flicker waits on tender hearts,
As hesitant as new moons' starts.
In shadows deep, where secrets hide,
Timid flames, with hope, abide.

Eyes meet shyly, a dance of light,
In the stillness of the night.
Burning softly, wary yet bold,
A story of love quietly told.

Breathless moments, a stolen glance,
Silent longing, a whispered chance.
In the warmth, two souls align,
A timid flame in sweet design.

Courage blooms like morning dew,
As hearts awaken, fresh and new.
From flicker to fire, we'll embrace,
Together we'll find our sacred space.

Nature's Confessions

Whispers float through rustling leaves,
Nature speaks, and softly grieves.
In quiet groves, secrets delight,
Confessions painted in moonlight.

Rivers hum their ancient song,
Through valleys wide, they glide along.
Mountains echo with tales of old,
In every stone, a dream is told.

The wind carries a gentle tune,
Under the watchful gaze of the moon.
Flowers bloom with colors bright,
Each petal speaks of love's pure light.

Listen close, the earth will share,
Her stories spun with utmost care.
In every breath, a truth is found,
In nature's heart, we're all unbound.

A Whispered Invitation

In twilight's glow, a whisper calls,
Through shadowed paths where silence falls.
An invitation soft and clear,
To dance with dreams, to draw you near.

Gentle winds will guide our way,
Across the night, where starlights play.
With every heartbeat, magic swells,
In the air, a story tells.

Beneath the sky, let spirits soar,
In timeless moments, forevermore.
With open hearts, we shall explore,
The whispered secrets, and so much more.

So take my hand; we'll leap beyond,
Into the night, where dreams respond.
A whispered path, our souls entwined,
In this sweet realm, love's pulse aligned.

Milton Keynes UK
Ingram Content Group UK Ltd.
UKHW021207261024
450281UK00007B/81